IN THE FRAME

GREAT RACING PHOTOGRAPHS

IN THE FRAME

GREAT RACING PHOTOGRAPHS

EDWARD WHITAKER

highdown

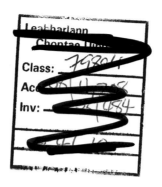
TO MY CHILDREN CHRISTOPHER AND OSCAR

Published in 2008 by Highdown,
an imprint of Raceform Ltd
Axis House, Compton, Newbury, Berkshire, RG20 6NL

ISBN 978-1-905156-49-8

Designed by Fiona Pike
Printed by Rotolito Lomarda, Italy

TITLE PAGE: TEOFILO AT JIM BOLGER'S STABLES, CO CARLOW, IRELAND.

CONTENTS

FOREWORD

I first met Edward Whitaker in 1987. He came into my office and explained with almost overbearing sincerity that for the *Racing Post* to progress it was absolutely essential that he, Edward, should be immediately equipped with the latest state-of-the-art camera on which, surprise, surprise, he already had an option. No change there then.

Such self belief in the young has its jagged edges and it was not long before there was a difficult but defining moment at Folkestone races when jockey Ray Goldstein took an ugly looking fall at the last fence. As others rushed over to help the ambulance men, Whitaker had the camera out. That night, with Goldstein happily recovered, we ran the picture in all its bloody gore. It told the story.

Over the years he has been the most prolific and creative of all the thorns that daily stick in an editor's side. During that time the jaggedness has eased a little but that hunger for images and eye for a story has never lessened. One evening last winter he rang up out of the blue. 'The forecast is snow,' he said, 'the first snow of the winter. I have booked into a B & B and looking down over Cheltenham from Cleeve Hill ought to make something special.'

Chris Smith has long been the 'Daddy' of all sports photographers. Edward has always aspired to be one of his sons. 'He has huge determination to get where the action is,' says Chris. 'And he also has a really good eye for a picture and that makes into a very formidable combination.'

Quite how formidable the following pages can testify. Racing is a many-faceted parish and *Racing Post* a multi-function news and publishing operation dedicated to serving all those who share its interest. Not least those who believe a great image can have a life beyond tomorrow's fish and chip wrappings. That's why we are proud of this book. That's why we are proud of Edward Whitaker.

Brough Scott
Racing Post Editorial Director 1987 – 2007

INTRODUCTION

It all started at the Badminton Horse Trials in 1978 – when I was 12. I had always had a passing interest in photography through my father's newspaper work as a Royal Correspondent, and I particularly enjoyed Badminton as we used to stay with a favourite aunt who lived in Nailsworth; I have loved the Cotswolds ever since.

At Badminton that year, Tim Graham, the famous royal photographer, lent me a Nikon F2 with a 180 mm/f2.8 lens and I trained my camera on the water jump in the cross country stage where poor Princess Anne duly crash landed. I was paid £30 for the sequence of the Princess going into the drink and it was published worldwide under Tim's name. It was my first photographic cheque and from then on I was determined to work as a newspaper photographer.

On the back of that I saved up for a Nikon FE and in the Sixth Form at school I started a Saturday job at John Rogers Sport and General agency in Exmouth Market, off the Farringdon Road. There I worked under the supervision of Jock McNee, and I mixed with photographers like Tim Bishop, Duncan Ridgely and John Ferguson. Sometimes I would be sent to a football match under the wing of Eddie Keogh and would develop black and white film, print the pictures and then drop them off at the different sports picture desks dotted around Fleet Street.

I was told to try and get on the photojournalism course in Sheffield where I won the Portfolio of The Year and during the time at college I did a couple of freelance jobs with the *Racing Post* which had just started. Then, after seven months travelling on the Indian subcontinent I came back and got myself a job with the *Racing Post*. My first assignment was photographing the great French filly Miesque winning the One Thousand Guineas at Newmarket in May 1987.

Twenty one years on I have been lucky enough to win the Racing Photographer of The Year four times and in 2006 was awarded Sports Journalist Association Award for Specialist Sports Portfolio. Those are the rewards but the challenge was and is to catch the images that are out there, and the way we operate now is almost unrecognizable from how it was at the beginning. Back in those way-before-digital days, we were shooting black and white film for the inside pages, and colour transparency for the front cover. The *Racing Post*, alongside the short lived *Today* newspaper, led the way with colour images on the front page and I am really proud to have been part of that. I was lucky enough to work alongside Gerry Cranham, Alan Johnson and Trevor Jones from whom I learnt a lot. Somehow they have put up with me as have some very talented and long suffering editors at the *Racing Post*. In their different ways Graham Rock, Michael Harris, Alan Byrne, Chris Smith and Bruce Millington have all been hugely supportive. When we started everything was done manually; exposing the film, focussing the lens and getting the pictures back to the office to meet the deadline. Nowadays we have the aid of autofocus and digital imagery to get a picture on the page without the process and printing stage. Out of everything the laptop computer has made it a lot easier for newspapers because we can now send pictures from anywhere with a connection. That said, the real key for a photographer is to see and anticipate a picture.

For me one of the great turning points was photographer Chris Smith's book *Sport in Focus* which I read just after I had joined the *Racing Post*. With Chris every picture was not just a striking image but told a story too. Suddenly I could see what I was trying to do. Other huge aids were racing photographers George Selwyn, Julian Herbert and the white bearded wonder that is Ed Byrne. In the wider field I have had the privilege to work near Bob Martin, Leo Mason, Hugh Routledge and Chris Smith himself. They have all helped but in the end it is just you and the camera trying to create a picture for others to enjoy.

I hope that these pages will prove that the process has not always been in vain.

Edward Whitaker
London 2008

SPRING

For a photographer spring is the time when everything quickens. New life arrives on the stud farms. In the jumping world all roads lead to Cheltenham and then on to Aintree, while on the Flat the gallops buzz and Classic dreams grow. I love spring because there is a feeling from the first foal onwards, that everyone has a chance. We move out of the darkness into light. It is a very exciting time.

A MARE AND FOAL

At the Ashford Stud in Versailles near Lexington, Kentucky. It was taken at first light. He was a lovely foal.

BIG DADDY AND SONS

Sadler's Wells, the greatest stallion of his era, is led out at Coolmore,
County Tipperary, followed by his descendants Galileo, Montjeu and
Hurricane Run.

THE KENTUCKY DAWN

A mare walks in front of one of the cathedral-like barns at Ashford.
I loved the gilded glow on the windows and the shimmer of the blue
grass beneath the mare.

COLOUR AND GALLOP COORDINATION

Three of trainer Luca Cumani's horses work over the Racecourse Side gallops at Newmarket. The Cumani string are always the most elegantly outfitted and I love the symmetry of this shot – everything is just perfectly balanced in terms of position, colour and light.

TOOLS OF THE TRADE

Persian Punch's groom Derek Brown stands inside a barn at
David Elsworth's yard at Whitsbury.

RETURNING FROM FIRST LOT

Trainer Barry Hills's horses – the group picture shows the horse as a
herd animal and you can see the spring in the new shoots on the trees.

A CLASSIC START

The Twin Spires of the Churchill Downs grandstand are the most iconic of all North American racing images. The picture is special because the horse in the nearest stall was withdrawn and I was able to position the camera in its place. I just love the power of this shot.

AT THE GALLOP

The Warren Hill all-weather track at Newmarket – with the town in the distance and the steepness of the incline very clear.

THE SPRING SKY

Hurdle race runners gallop on the skyline at Wincanton racecourse
in Somerset.

McCoy Goes Formula One

Teetotal champion jockey AP McCoy shakes the champagne at
Warwick racecourse on 2 April 2002 to celebrate a new record
of 270 winners in a single season. His final total was 289.

McCoy Does Hurt

The champion jockey covers up after being fired into the turf on a horse
called Snowy Morning in the Hennessy Gold Cup at Newbury in 2007.

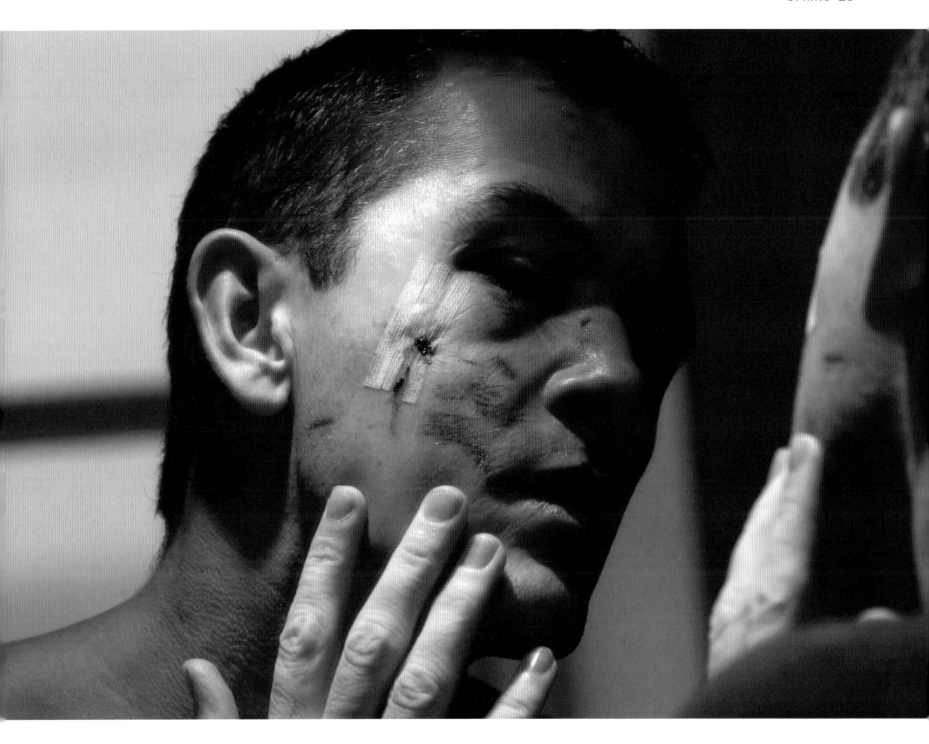

THE SCARS OF THE GAME

AP McCoy looks at his battered face in the mirror. It didn't stop him riding for long.

SUNRISE AT CHELTENHAM

Trainer Willie Mullins' horses exercise on the gallops in the middle of the track. This was on the Monday morning of the 2007 Cheltenham Festival.

BETTING REFLECTIONS AT NEWBURY

Working as a bookmaker can be a damp profession – and the punters
didn't look too dry either.

THE START AT LINGFIELD

This is the seven furlong start at the very top of the straight and having just three runners made the perfect frame for this picture.

RUBY'S ROAR

Ruby Walsh screams at the sky after winning the Queen Mother
Champion Chase on Azertyuiop.

A CHAMPION'S LEAP

AP McCoy on Acambo (grey) jumps the first fence in a beginners' chase
at Ascot, November 2007.

FACING THE STARTER

Spring sunshine catches the runners at the tapes at Cheltenham.

THE BEST MATE MOMENT

Trainer Henrietta Knight and husband Terry Biddlecombe are
overcome with emotions after their horse (light blue colours)
has won his third consecutive Gold Cup.

KICKING KING

The 2005 Gold Cup was his and Barry Geraghty's hour.
I have seen many jockeys in their moment of triumph, but
none so cool as Geraghty. The horse looked pretty chuffed too.

THE PAUL NICHOLLS THREE HANDER

The trainer stands at home at Manor Farm Stables, Ditcheat in
Somerset with the horses he had saddled to take the first three
places in the previous day's Gold Cup at Cheltenham. From the left
– runner-up Kauto Star, winner Denman and third Neptune Collonges.

TWO GOLD CUP WINNERS IN THE STREET

2008 hero Denman (Sam Thomas, left) and 2007 victor Kauto Star
(Ruby Walsh, right) walk through their local village of Ditcheat in
Somerset.

THE QUIET BEFORE THE STORM

American champion Pleasantly Perfect exercises before winning the 2004 Dubai World Cup later in the week. I love the change of rhythm and culture immediately after Cheltenham.

THE UNVEILING OF THE TROPHY

The cover is lifted from the Dubai World Cup at the front of the royal
box at Nad al Sheba. The image is an ultimate Arabian Night.

REFLECTIONS

Ginger McCain will ever be associated with triple Grand National winner Red Rum, pictured behind him. But this photo was taken after he trained Amberleigh House to win in 2004, 27 years after Red Rum's final victory.

LEADING THE NATIONAL

Eventual winner Silver Birch (far right with white noseband) jumps the water jump with a circuit to go before his and Robbie Power's triumph in the 2007 Grand National.

THE GRAND NATIONAL CAVALRY CHARGE

The six fence gallop down to Becher's Brook – 2007 saw the opening of the new grandstand which gave me this fresh vantage point for one of the classic sporting moments of the year.

Buttercups at Bath

Horses spin past my low set camera at the Somerset track in May
to give us a mole's eye view.

THE GATES SLAM OPEN AT LINGFIELD

The camera is bolted to the upright of the starting stalls and takes us
inside the moment when the race explodes into life.

A LAP TO GO ON THE ROODEYE

Hugs Dancer (no 6) tracks the leaders before going on to win the
Chester Cup in 2003.

GATEWAY TO GLORY

Even the lowliest race like this little one at Lingfield is victory for
someone. The empty starting stalls on the right set up this image
for me.

A FRENCH CONVERSATION

Champion jockey Christophe Soumillon (second left) holds court before
winning at Saint-Cloud. The racing scene has a much more relaxed feel
out there – and I think this picture personifies it.

BETFRED.com
BETFRED.com
TRIPLEPRINT
DOUBLEPRINT
skybet 08000 722 421
BETFRED.com
BETFRED.com
BETFRED.com

GRASS STRIPES

A breathtaking aerial image of the runners fighting out the finish in the opening race at Sandown in April 2004. Tony McCoy on board Mondial Jack (right) wins.

SHOWER FOR A SIRE

Danehill, the star stallion at Coolmore. I was photographing the
2,000 Guineas winner Rock of Gibraltar when his father Danehill
came by to be hosed down right by us. Just how much he loved the
spray you can see in the picture.

SUMMER

Summertime may not make the living easier for photographers but it certainly helps them with the light – some stables are on the move as early as 5am and there is magic in those mornings. High summer brings us the big days at Ascot and Epsom – but I like the wild ones too.

A THREE HORSE GALLOP ON THE LIMEKILNS

This is the most evocative of all the Newmarket gallops and the two trees made the perfect frame for this trio of Godolphin horses on a summer morning.

A THUNDER SKY AT CARTMEL

The Lake District track in Cumbria has weather of many moods.
I have never seen it quite as mixed as this.

LADY IN RED

A lone scarlet 'Turfiste' watches the action at a sodden Goodwood
in May.

THE BREAK AT BRIGHTON

Runners leap out of the stalls at the mile and a half start at Brighton,
the furthest point from the grandstand and high on the Sussex Downs.

A SALISBURY QUINTET

Five runners stretch out across this Wiltshire downland track with
the famous cathedral spire identifying it in the background.

Motivator's Derby 2005

I had been following Motivator's training right through the season and was so convinced he would win that I got permission to set up on the top of the Queen's Stand looking down at this extraordinary winner's circle.

DETTORI'S DERBY

Frankie Dettori winning on Authorized in 2007. He had waited 20
years to win the Derby and when it came it was truly spectacular.

OUIJA BOARD WINS THE OAKS

Ouija Board poses for the cameras after winning in 2004. What intrigued me about the picture is the bearded, grey-suited figure looking on up on the right – Sheikh Mohammed!

2006 SIR PERCY'S DERBY

A four way photo finish, the closest Derby ever and as luck would have it I had put a camera under the rail on the line. Sir Percy is closest to it and inched it off, from right, Dylan Thomas, Dragon Dancer and Hala Bek.

THE ODDEST OBSTACLE OF THEM ALL

The lake crossing on the steeplechase track at Hamburg. It involves
100 metres of actual swimming and on this occasion the horse one
from the right was so good in the water that he reached the bank with
an unassailable lead.

SOLAR ECLIPSE

Lambourn August 1999 – a multiple exposure shot taken every
ten minutes of the 96% total solar eclipse.

THE ROYAL ASCOT COACH

It may be traditional but to see this close up in Ascot High Street
is always a wonder.

THE ROYAL ASCOT COACH

Limo style. I was up in a helicopter photographing the new grandstand
and suddenly was hit by this image. In many ways it is symbolic of the
ostentatious side of racing in 2006.

A TIGHT FINISH

Galileo (left) beats Fantastic Light in the 2001 King George VI and
Queen Elizabeth Stakes at Ascot. This is my favourite Flat race
finish. Two great horses and fine jockeys duelling, Ballydoyle versus
Godolphin, Kinane v Dettori. They locked up into a duel and the
three year old Galileo just prevailed. It was terrific.

THE RACE IS RUN

Pulling-up after the Totesport International on King George day at
Ascot 2007 – the winner, Third Set, is clear at the top right but I love
the stream of defeated cavalry that the rest of the runners suggest.

SILHOUETTES AT ROYAL ASCOT

The outlines against the coming storm were so good that I took the
colour out of the frame.

HIGH FASHION ON LADIES' DAY

We have never met but I couldn't resist these autumn colours
in the height of summer.

A PASSING ON THE STAIRS

Ian McEwan could write a whole novel about this. What happened next? Did they really never speak? Royal Ascot deserves the book.

ROYAL TRAPPINGS

For a people-watcher Ascot never ceases to amaze.

BUTTERFLY WOMAN

Great hat and you should see her face!

ILL-MANNERED CELEBRATION

The excesses of jockey gestures were bound to lead to silliness like
this from Christophe Soumillon after winning the King George on
Hurricane Run in 2006.

GLORIOUS GOODWOOD

High summer on the Sussex Downs as seen from the Sussex Stand –
no setting in racing can be more perfect than this.

MOMENT OF RELEASE

Elhamri and Richard Kingscote (yellow colours) break from the stalls on
their way to winning over the downhill five furlong track at Goodwood.

BATTLESHIP SKY AT NEWMARKET

As the runners launch up the July Course with the Devil's Dyke beside
them the sky gave us this three dimensional effect.

STAG PARTY SCOOP6

The bonus winners seem quite pleased with the horse they backed at Doncaster – they had landed £ 227,840 between them!

DUEL IN THE SUN

Light Shift (right) and Sweet Lilly duel at the finish of the Nassau
Stakes at Goodwood 2007.

STREETS AT DEAUVILLE

This looks like a road crossing but is actually an image facing down from the track into what remains the most stylish of all racing holiday towns.

LES GRANDES ECURIES AT CHANTILLY

This astonishing doorway reflects the best story in French racing, how the 18th century Prince de Condé was so convinced he would be reincarnated as a horse that he built this horse chateau to ensure that in the next life he would live as he had been accustomed to.

A DIP AT DEAUVILLE

Racehorses walking in the sea every morning is one of the loveliest
sights I know.

SHARP LINES AT YORK

This was at the 2007 Ebor Meeting and produced a symmetry of people, horses and shadows that has never been bettered.

INTO THE STRAIGHT AT LONGCHAMP

This shot of the runners swinging off the final turn points us towards
the autumn; the mirrored towers of the backdrop are of La Défense.

LE VIEUX MOULIN

The Old Windmill at Longchamp is so perfectly camouflaged amongst the trees that only the horses show you are just yards from the racecourse stands in the very centre of Paris.

AUTUMN

Autumn gives us a natural end to the Flat racing scene and leads into the National Hunt season proper. By the end of the summer we are getting a bit weary of Flat racing although we do of course have the joys of the Breeders' Cup trip to come. To suddenly be thinking of trips down to Somerset to see Paul Nicholls and his team quickens the pulse every time. Technically it comes a bit harder because of the light but when you do get the sunny days and that autumn tint it can all be worth it.

FRANKIE'S FAREWELL

Frankie Dettori salutes the gilded winning post in Ascot's old victory enclosure to which he returned a record seven times on that golden day in 1996.

OUT OF THE MIST

Jonjo O'Neill's horses headed by Black Jack Ketchum come up the
gallops at Jackdaws Castle with the autumn mist lying in the valley.

THE WATER JUMP AT EXETER

The tint of the light on the leaves and on the water gives that exact autumn feel.

AUTUMN COLOURS AT CHEPSTOW

The late sun (and the seagull) transform this shot.

NEWMARKET DAWN

Horses on the Rowley Mile on the morning of Champions Day in
October 2006.

THE BATTLE OF THE ARC

Montjeu beats Japanese star El Condor Pasa in the 1999 Prix de l'Arc de Triomphe. I love the leverage and the power in Montjeu's hindquarters.

GOODWOOD IN SEPTEMBER

It's a very different light than high summer. Runners and riders at the
farthest point of the racecourse.

COWBOYS

Lone Star Park, Texas – horses readying for the 2004 Breeders' Cup.

SUNRISE AT BELMONT

Hope in the morning, wherever you are.

ARAZI AND JOCKEY PAT VALENZUELA TAKE OFF

This victory in the 1991 Breeders' Cup Juvenile at Churchill Downs
is hailed as one of the greatest performances ever seen and getting
this image was a formative moment in my own career. It was my first
Breeders' Cup – it would not be my last.

GETTING READY

Royal Anthem and Gary Stevens exercise before the Breeders' Cup
at Gulfstream Park, Florida, November 1999.

DAWN AT SANTA ANITA

That early California sun . . .

THE BREAK FROM THE GATE

The start of the Breeders' Cup Juvenile at Santa Anita, November 1993.

THE VINDICATION LEAP

Frankie Dettori's ecstatic flying dismount after winning the 1999
Breeders' Cup Turf on Daylami, 12 months after his much criticised
defeat on Swain in the Classic at Churchill Downs.

MUD AT MONMOUTH

The 2007 Breeders' Cup at Monmouth Park was the wettest ever
– Frankie Dettori leads on Kelly's Landing in the Sprint.

MUD GLORIOUS MUD

Frankie Dettori's wry expression belies the hardship of racing under
testing conditions.

ARLINGTON

Michael Kinane – even four visors can't help resist the perils of dirt racing in the USA.

SCHOOLING MORNING

Jockeys are switched on trainer Nicky Henderson's horses at Seven Barrows at Lambourn.

AUTUMN STROLL

Trainer Ian Balding takes Moor Cottage (and his dogs) for a walk up the Kingsclere avenue.

WINTER

Winter brings water – and anything to do with water and horses, whether it be frost, mud, snow or rain, makes great images. Obviously there is not much light but it creates the mood and often gives us that cold, bluey light which emphasises the earthiness of the horse racing game. All these seasons are about the light and we are so lucky to have these very different seasons in Britain.

And once we have had the shortest day in December there is the promise of gradually increasing light all the way to the Cheltenham Festival and then on into the Flat racing summer. Changing seasons – but new delights.

A FROSTY MORNING

Nicky Henderson's horses return to their stables at Seven Barrows amidst the Berkshire Downs.

TWINNED LEGENDS

Lester Piggott, then 61, rides Desert Orchid, then 18, in a charity
parade at Wincanton Racecourse in 1997. It was the only time the
two icons were ever together.

THE JUMPING COLOSSUS

Denman crossing the fourth last fence at Newbury in February 2007,
his first season as a chaser.

THE NEW BROOM

When Martin Pipe handed over to his son David in 2006 he was never
going to just sit around. Having his bike propped against the wall only
added to the restlessness of the image.

PORTRAIT ON THE SCALES

Ruby Walsh in the weighing room at Newbury.

STORM AND THE ROCK

Stallion Rock of Gibraltar walks as the sun comes out on a rain-soaked Coolmore.

STUDYING FORM

This may look posed but it wasn't. As ever at Cheltenham it is the
backdrop that makes it.

THE FLYING DISMOUNT

Carl Llewellyn being thrown off at Warwick – the impact of hitting a
fence hard shows beautifully in the scattering birch (left) and the flying
whip (right).

RED SKY IN THE MORNING

There is something eternal in this picture of Jim Best's horses shot on
the old Lewes racecourse, high on the South Downs in Sussex.

MICK FITZGERALD

'Mick Fitz' did 20 years as a jockey before retiring in 2008. You can see
how he liked to be immaculate.

THE BIG STAND-OFF

Hoo La Baloo and Ruby Walsh reach for the open ditch at Sandown.

BIRCH FLIES AT FONTWELL

This mole's eye view comes from my remote control-operated camera
facing the low winter sun.

ALL WEATHER EFFORT AT KEMPTON

The grip of the jockeys' toes and the whirl of the horses' hooves gives
the sense of tension and speed.

WINTER'S LEAP

Steeplechasing silhouettes against the setting sun at Warwick.

Night Racing at Kempton

The horses seem to be running in emptiness. With Kempton's small crowds, that has sometimes been a bit near the actual truth.

NIGHT RACING AT HAPPY VALLEY

'Emptiness' is not a word we ever associate with Hong Kong.
I remember the roar from the stands as I took this picture.

JUMPS SUPERSTARS

AP McCoy and Ruby Walsh with goggles down before the start at Cheltenham.

THE LAUNCH OF THE OPEN

The runners for the first race leave the start at Cheltenham's Open Meeting in November.

Heavy Weather

The horse Heavy Weather leads at Fontwell – no winner was ever
better named.

THEY BOTH WALKED AWAY

Some people objected when this shot of Dave Crosse and Saint
Godegrand somersaulting at Chepstow was made the lead picture
on the Injured Jockeys Fund Calendar for 2007. But the picture shows
the risks taken – and proof that you can overcome them.

HOPE ON THE FELLS

Hennessy Gold Cup hope Kingsmark (Dianne Mosley, right) walks
home to his Lake District stables with the mist shrouded Shap Fells
as a backdrop.

COLD IN THE COTSWOLDS

A midwinter picture of Jonjo O'Neill's horses at Jackdaws Castle near Stow-on-the-Wold.

FEEL YOUR FINGERS

This was not a morning to be without gloves.

A SNOWY MEMORY

Best Mate – the much loved triple Gold Cup winner and a sweatered-up
Jackie Jenner in the lanes near Lockinge, Oxfordshire.

THE BUZZARD AFTER THE BLIZZARD

Newmarket under snow always looks spectacular but the buzzard above
the gallopers made this picture unique.

ACKNOWLEDGEMENTS

In addition to those I have already thanked in my Introduction there are others I must mention.

Firstly, to the equine and human subjects of my photographs. Though the images are largely celebrating horseracing sometimes you have to record the downside and I thank those for their understanding of this.

Secondly to the many professionals I am lucky enough to work with: The brilliance of the subeditors particularly Nick Barnes and Paul Crabtree on the *Racing Post* whose clever headlines and layout techniques have made my pictures stand out on the page. The picture desk led by the very brave David Cramphorn and to his team for their great skills in making my pictures look good on newsprint. In addition to my former picture editor Jon Winter for his truly amazing vision and talents.

Also the team at Highdown, particularly Julian Brown and Fiona Pike for putting the book together.

To my favourite photographer Chris Smith for all his help in collecting and selecting the pictures both for the exhibition and the book.

My thanks for the inspiration I have received from the journalists throughout my career. In particular Colin Mackenzie, Richard Edmondson, Paul Hayward, Paul Haigh, Andrew Longmore, Julian Muscat and above all Brough Scott whose unremitting support has always been there.

Finally and most importantly, my thanks to my family; Mum and Dad, my brother Thomas, my sister Victoria, grandparents Krysia and Norman, to Eva and Henry, 8, and particularly my wonderful children Christopher, 10, and Oscar 7 who make everything seem worthwhile.